Winnetka-Northfield Public Library

3 1240 00553 1194

DEC - 2016

WITHDRAWN

My First Dog: A Guide To Caring

For Your New Best Friend

WINNETKA-NORTHFIELD
PUBLIC LIBRARY DISTRICT
WINNETKA, IL 60093
847-446-7220

© June 2016, Teddy O'Malley

Cover by izinkkas via Pixabay.com under the CC0 licence.

All interior photography © Angie Dickens.

Are you ready for a dog?

There are a few things to consider before you decide to get a dog. Are you ready for one? You might be thinking yes, yes, yes!

But let's not get ahead of ourselves.

Dogs require time and money. Do you have space in your yard for a dog to run and play? If not, will you take him for long walks to make up for it? Are you willing to potty train your new pet? Potty training can be a slow and frustrating process. Would you be mad if someone ate your homework or your toys?

Dogs can live for eighteen years or longer. This means that getting a dog is a long-term decision.

Who will be paying for the new puppy's things?

Will you pay with your allowance or will your parents be paying? Will the dog belong to you, your parents, or everyone in the family?

There are many things to think about before you decide to get a new pet.

Dog or Puppy?

This is something you should think about carefully. Dogs are active and need to go outside for walks. Puppies are even more active.

A puppy will need more training than an older dog. The puppy will also be teething. His teeth will be growing in. This might mean that he chews on things that he is not supposed to. It could even be your toy or your homework. As cliché as it sounds, my first family dog did eat my homework!

A puppy may also take longer to potty train. You will need to teach your puppy to go to the bathroom outside or in a designated area such as on newspaper. Your puppy will need to learn many new things!

Another possible option to consider is getting a senior dog. You might get a few less years with a senior dog, but they are not rowdy and you don't have to worry about teething. Senior dogs are often potty trained. The biggest effort with a senior dog is helping her adjust to her new home with you.

Consider making a list of what you want and expect from your new pet. This will help you decided whether a dog or puppy is right for you. Whatever you do, don't get a puppy because they are cuter. All puppies become dogs.

Picking a breed

If you are wanting something specific in a dog, then you may want to consider picking a breed or two. Keep in mind that regardless of breed, each dog has their own unique personality.

But some breeds are known for being more energetic while others are more placid. Some are considered friendly while others are not. Some breeds have long hair while others have short hair. You can find websites with dog breeds and even quizzes that will help you decide which dog breed is right for you. You shouldn't make your ultimate decision based on an internet quiz. But it could definitely be useful. And it's fun. This leads us to our next section.

Buy or Adopt?

There are those on both sides of the fence. Some say buying is fine if you want a specific breed of dog, and for that reason they go to a breeder to get their dog.

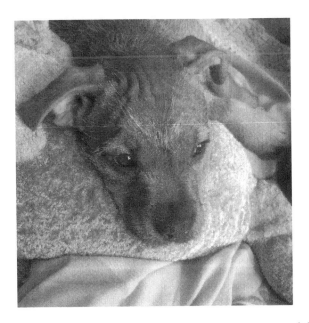

Others are strong advocates of adoption and don't believe in buying dogs at all. This is because there are many overcrowded animal shelters and adopting is part of the solution. You can find purebred dogs in a shelter if you look, or in some cases, get on a waiting list. But a mutt may steal your heart while you are looking!

Where can I get a dog or puppy?

There are a few places where you can get a dog or puppy.

- The newspaper
- From a friend who is giving them away
- From an animal shelter
- From a breeder
- From a classified ad or internet group

Often people give away pets

they can no longer take care of in the

newspaper. You can also check your

local online classified ads. There are many Facebook groups dedicated to re-homing pets and puppies. You may even find one in your local area. Some of these sites allow breeders to post as well.

Supplies

You will need some basic supplies before you get your new dog or puppy. A food and water bowl, a bed, and a crate or baby gate. You will want to keep a new puppy out of certain areas and out of trouble. The baby gate or crate is useful for this.

Other things you will need for your new pet.

Identification

Toys

Grooming Supplies (such as brush, comb, shampoo, conditioner)

If you adopt a puppy, he will
need to be vaccinated if his former

owner has not had it done already. Your puppy will need various vaccines and boosters from the age of six weeks up to the age of fourteen weeks. Talk to your vet about which vaccines your new puppy will need and when. If you've adopted an older dog, then you may still need to look into having him vaccinated for Rabies.

Picking That Special Dog

Some people take a while to bond to their dog. Others fall in love with their pet the moment they first lay eyes on them.

When looking at pets at a place such as the shelter, make sure to look over all the pets. Is there one you keep going back to pet? Is there one you can't take your mind off of no matter how many others you look at? This is probably the one!

If you find your special pet online, then you might want to arrange a meet-and-greet with the owner. Make sure your parents or guardians go with you. Never go to meet someone you don't know alone!

Naming Your Dog

Naming your dog can be a fun, silly, or special experience. Some people go with their dog's looks. Brownie is brown. Oreo is black and white. Spot has a big spot around his eye or perhaps on his butt! Lucky was saved from the shelter right before her time was up.

Don't feel that you have to limit yourself to basic dog names, though. There are many cute ones such as Fluffy, Fido, Rover, Brownie, Oreo, and Max. There are lots of other options as well. You can use this as a chance to be original and go with something like Mr. Bojangles, Noodles, or Pancake.

You could also use it as a chance to give a name that you love. Maybe you've always been fond of Sasha, Lola, or Haley. This is a chance to use that favorite name!

There are many sites that can help you find pet or baby names on the internet and in libraries. So take a look around or just have your friends and family toss out names until you hear one that you love.

Grooming A Short Haired Dog

Brush your dog's coat gently or use a shedding mitten to help reduce shedding.

To clean your dog's face, gently wipe with a lukewarm washcloth. Do not pull on any dirt that might be near your dog's eye. Continue gently rubbing until the dirt is removed.

Grooming A Long Haired Dog

Carefully brush out your dog's hair. Now run a comb through to get out any tangles. Be careful not to pull the hair.

Clean the eyes the same way. But gently comb out any tangled hair near their eyes.

Potty Training

Potty training your new pet can be a frustrating experience. It can be made worse or better depending on how you react to your pet. If your new pet has an accident, do not strike your pet. Do not rub your pet's nose in it. Do not get angry. This is normal.

You were once a baby and could not control your bladder and bowels. The puppy is a baby as well. He doesn't know better. Keep calm and take your puppy outside. Tell the puppy "no" and get him quickly out the door and into the yard.

You will need to take your new dog or puppy out often to avoid accidents. Take him out after a meal and when he wakes up in the morning. Be patient. Sometimes you might have to sit outside for a while before your puppy feels the urge to go. Sometimes your puppy will go as soon as you bring him back in. Don't get upset. Simply take the puppy back outside to try again.

Make sure to reward your puppy when he does pee or poop outside. You can tell him, "Good potty", so that he will associate the word "potty" with going outside.

The most important part of potty training is to be patient. Your puppy will get it soon enough!

Paper Training

Paper training may be right for you if you have a small dog or you live in an apartment. It can be handy for when you are gone at school as well.

Paper training will train your dog to go potty in a specific area, so only put paper where you want your dog to potty.

When your puppy starts sniffing as if she has to potty, take her to the paper and try to keep her in the area until she goes. This may take a few times. Sometimes she will walk away seeming as if she doesn't have to go, and then potty. Try not to get frustrated. She isn't being mischievous on purpose. She just needs your time and patience.

PART II

TRAINING AND TRICKS

Teaching Simple Commands

There are a few simple commands that will come in handy. They could even save your dog's life! Because some of these commands are easier done with a name, I will use my dog, Sasha, for the example.

Come!

Start by moving a few feet away from your dog.

Say, "Sasha, come!" or "Come here, Sasha!"

When Sasha comes to you, reward her by petting her and saying, "Good dog, Sasha!"

Stay!

This one is a little more difficult, especially if your dog tends to follow you everywhere. It could save your dog from getting out into the street or running away, though.

It's best to teach your dog this command early.

Say, "Stay, Sasha!"

Walk a few feet away from her. It might take a few tries, but soon Sasha will stay. When Sasha stays, say, "Good stay,".

Go to her and then shower her with affection as a reward.

Sit!

This one is easier to teach if you have a treat, though it isn't totally necessary.

Start by saying, "Sasha, sit!"
Then gently push down on Sasha's bottom.
If Sasha sits, say, "Good sit, Sasha."
If Sasha resists, simply do not give her the reward.
Be patient and try again.
Do not get angry with your dog. She just doesn't understand you.

Lie Down

Say, "Lie Down, Sasha!"

Gently lower Sasha into a lying position.

Reward her.

Keep doing this until Sasha lies down on her own.

Try not to get impatient. This one may take a few tries.

Go to your room or Kennel Up!

This is a helpful command if you need to put your dog up in a room or kennel while you are gone so that they do not get into things. If you do not have a kennel, then you might consider putting your dog in the bathroom while you're away. She will have room to stretch her legs. And you won't have to worry about her chewing on your books or pooping in your chair.

Say, "Go to your room, Sasha!" and take a treat into the room that you would like Sasha to enter.

If using a kennel, say "Kennel up!" and toss the treat into the kennel.

Once Sasha enters, say, "Good girl, Sasha!"

Smile so that Sasha knows you are pleased with her and close the door.

Fun Tricks

If your dog is good at learning commands, then perhaps it's time to teach her a few fun tricks!

Shake!

This one is easier than you might think.

Tell your dog, "Sasha, shake!" Reward any movement of the paw. You may need to practice a few times. When Sasha puts her paw in your hand, say, "Good shake!" and reward her with either praise or treats.

High-Five!

Once you've taught "Shake", it becomes easy to teach high-five.

Say, "High five!" and hold your hand out flat.
If Sasha taps your hand with her paw, say, "Good girl, Sasha! Good high-five!" and reward her with praise or treats.

Roll Over

This is one trick that isn't really necessary to teach your dog, but it is adorable! It will be easier if your dog knows the command, "Lie Down" first.

Say, "Sasha, lie down!"

Once Sasha lies down, say, "Roll over, Sasha!"

Move the treat in front of Sasha's face from one side to the other. Sasha will roll in the direction of the treat.

Sometimes Sasha might try to get back up. Don't sweat it. Just try again later.

To teach Roll Over without a treat:

Say, "Lie down, Sasha!"

If Sasha lies down, say, "Roll over, Sasha!"

Then nudge Sasha until she has rolled.

Reward her.

"Good girl, Sasha. Good roll over!"

Part III – LOVING YOUR DOG

This might be the shortest part of the book, but it's also the most important. Love your dog unconditionally. Aside from feeding and walking your dog, you'll want to pet, play with, and talk to your dog on a regular basis. This is great for both of you!

**Check out other books
by Teddy O'Malley**

Cool Kids Wear Glasses

The Fairy's Bubble Wand

Destiny And Faith Go To Twincentric
Academy

Destiny and Faith's Summer
Adventures

Destiny And Faith Get Stuck In The
Country

MY NOTES

64929680R00029

Made in the USA
Charleston, SC
12 December 2016